Creativity

With Spiritual Lynx

By Heather Leigh

Creativity With Spiritual Lynx

Text © 2021 Heather Leigh

Leigh, Heather

Creativity With Spiritual Lynx / Heather Leigh

Also by Heather Leigh

Juvenile Fiction

Hey Little Baby
Scout and Ellie, The Birthday Party
Scout and Ellie, the Beauty Pageant
Scout and Ellie, The Ski Resort
Scout and Ellie, The Giraffe Next Door
Scout and Ellie, To Be Santa
What Piper Peppertree Found

Pre-Teen Paranormal Trilogy

Red Nectar
Black Licorice
Suicide Soda

Non-Fiction

Are You An Intelligent Massage Therapist?
Are You An Intelligent Mover?
Own Your Massage
What Kind Of Peanut Butter Is Your Massage?

<u>Blogs</u>
<u>www.heatherleighauthor.blogspot.com</u>
<u>www.spirituallynx.blogspot.com</u>

Table of Contents

Chapter Eight

Now, Let's Create Something

Introduction

Creativity is the imagination come to life, the power within to create something enticing. It is original, shakes the mind, and showcases the fascinating side of everything. It is being in, and experiencing, the grace of God.

Like creativity, we are distinct. Our life experiences, viewpoints, cultural influencers, sexual orientation, skin color, bodies, and upbringing are all varied, one from another. Our unique, individual presence is required to keep the world spinning at precisely the correct speed. If you were not here, the balance would be off. You are needed here.

We're born to be creative, that's the reason we're here. We come to life with wonder, enthusiasm, and a readiness to express as no one has before us. When left unhindered, we are fresh with ideas, pumping with innovation, and an impulse to plug our creativity into the world. Why else would the earth be flush in variety if not for us to add to it?

Creativity, we were born with it. It is our default mode.

Growing up, I attended eight different elementary schools, two middle schools, and five high schools. I have lived in ten different cities in California, from the southern border to the Pacific Northwest. Four states, four countries.

This may sound like a crazy, untethered life. But the variety of viewpoints is refreshing. It shook me up to learn the resourceful way each place adapted to their environment. I am thankful for the creativity I experienced in every place I have lived.

What I came to realize is that what is accepted as the norm in one community can be unacceptable behavior in another. Jokes often make no sense in a different culture. Parenting norms are inconsistent. Men and women interactions and expectations vary.

In review of my life, I am proud of my use of creativity. It is something that has added value to my life. I use creativity to:

- expand writing venues
- bring more joy to my life
- attempt to be a better mother
- enhance my spiritual journey
- explore new activities

As allowing creativity to seep into my life, I hope to let it spill from me to you in this book. I yearn to present to you the value of being creative, obstacles that may block it, and how to let it enrich your life. And, keep a spiritual mist that will flow throughout.

When my father visited Yellowstone National Park, he was captivated with the herds of wild horses. They were full of life, fresh, free, unburdened. They lived as a healthy community that savored individuality. Creativity is like a wild horse, and you are one of them.

God/Goddess will be used interchangeably throughout this book. God is the highest vibration that the Spiritual Lynx is attempting to link you with. If you think of yourself as a drop of sunlight, goddess would be a bundle of all suns. A drop of water to an infinite ocean. A star in a universe that never ends. In this way, we are connected to one another and a part of goddess.

This book is offered in two ways of reading. First, it can be read straight through from chapter to chapter. Second, each section can, for the most part, stand alone. You can pick and choose what topic to meander through. Join the Spiritual Lynx in prowling into your creative spirit!

Chapter One
Benefits of Creativity

In picking up this book, you have expressed an interest in creativity. But the effort of reading through it and applying the knowledge to your life must be met with some gains. Or else, why bother? So, let's start with the basics of why the pursuit of being more creative is an asset.

Brings Life-Long Joy

Before my son could crawl, I put socks with bells on to his feet and stood back to watch. Laying on his back, kicking his legs, the bells rang. He pumped his arms in excitement. His legs kicked again, again the sound. A third time, it happened again. And I watched that little face change into comprehension. He kicked his legs and a wondrous sound was heard. He had made the connection: his actions caused an effect. He created a noise.

His world opened up. No longer was he a helpless being, waiting for an outsider to make right his universe. He could create a sound that brought him joy. What else could he create? What could his arms, hands, legs do? Could they move where he wanted them to? Could his hands scratch his own nose? Feet kick a toy hanging over him?

These questions were beyond his thought processes at his few months old self. But the realization was a seed in a lifetime of discovering of what he is capable. The ability to create music from merely kicking was a huge leap of consciousness.

The profundity of this realization gave way to joy. He was fascinated with his discovery.

You have that ability to create. The more you realize that you are your prime architect, the more joy you can bring to your life. You can still feel that joy in creating that starts from the moment you realized are a creator. From childhood play to a new idea at work, the happiness in being an originator can be felt every day. You have the ability to generate your own contented, splendiferous life.

Persistent Variety Show

We are born into a world that begs us to create. Our surroundings implore, plead, snatch at our minds to add zest to it. Want proof? Look the variety around you. All of the gadgets, decorations, and mugs of coffee are made from different materials. The filament in a lightbulb, innards of a reading device, clothing fabrics, residue of hand soap. People put together all of these materials, mashed them into products for you.

If those people came up with things we can utilize and enjoy, then you can do the same. Don't freak out. Don't feel overwhelmed. You don't have to forge a product that others will utilize. Your stuff could be a craft that no one but your friends ever see. It is not always the production but rather the gratification of fabricating that is the important point.

Creations don't stop with physical things. Ideas are creative, too. Democracy, freedom, communication, me running a marathon (this is listed as an idea because it's just never going to happen). You just sitting in a room and thinking can become an idea that can eventually be shared.

We can use things for their intended purpose, or discover new ways to use the same old thing. Our minds are not in lock-down mode when it comes to repurposing. The cloth I keep on my desk to chase away the dust bunnies is currently serving as a coaster for a mug of ice water, keeping those stain inducing water rings away from the wood desk. Okay, that is a mini re-purpose. Just think of the bigger things that can find other uses. All it takes is a bit of creative thought. Eyesore of an old car in your drive-way? Donate it. Big plastic cup from Starbucks? Water pitcher for a flower pot.

With all of this variety we are subjected to, we get to add to it, be a part of it, receive and dish it out. Bathe in the bubbles of endless variety.

<u>Great Soup Contributor</u>

We all contribute our special flavor of creativity to the Great Soup of Life. Every human being has their world view, little microcosms of intake that cannot be repeated by another. You are one of those beings, everything about you is unique. Every experience that you have, every event, every incident is perceived from a perspective completely different from each other. You can taste a ripe summer peach and your taste buds will behold the sweetness in a wham-bam way that is your personal secret.

Another whoop to the wash of fun is that your neighbor gets to contribute their learnings as well. We can all benefit from different viewpoints. Great soup is prime when all are allowed to contribute.

You don't have to accept every addition; if your brother adds radishes and you detest them, you can pluck out that red root from your bowl. But please, don't throw it in his face. Probably best to feed it to a hungry rabbit. And, of course, ingredients of fear or ignorance, chuck out that stuff, too.

Mmm, think I'll go heat up some soup for dinner.

Blast World Challenges

We have many tough world problems: climate change, economic issues, hunger, wars, racism. A Pandora's box of issues. They cling together like a thousand sailor's knots lurking in a sunken pirate ship. It's easy to be so overcome with life challenges that a Why Even Try Attitude can creep into our thoughts. Rather than becoming the ostrich with its head in the sand, remember creativity.

There are innovations seeking to reduce climate change. A new technology utilizing huge intake fans suck out carbon dioxide from the air. That carbon dioxide is what makes your soda fizz. And, there is too much of it in our air from human pollutants— cars and factories. The captured gas can be used for energy. Now that is creativity problem solving in action.

What creative solutions have you seen to earth's challenges?

It doesn't have to be as big as a carbon sucking mega fan. Plogging is a new exercise trend of jogging and picking up trash along the way. Cardio and lunges in the same workout. Easy breezy lemon pie squeezy. That is, if you're a runner.

- If you have errands to run this week, create a roadway puzzle. A gaming path of ways to get as much done as possible within each outing. Limiting car usage lessens car exhaust.
- Used clothes are filling up our landfills. Have a clothing swap night with friends—wine, laughter and a new-to-you wardrobe in one night.
- Throw a party with the entrance fee being a donation to a local charity.

The earth is pleading for attention. New ways of doing things are needed for the troubles in our world. Solutions are out there. For every poison, there are antidotes to weaken its blow. Mark a compartment in your brain for ways to contribute. The more people with those tucked-in, ready-to-use compartments, the better off we all are.

Jubilant Friendships

There is too much to experience, contribute and feel in the world for one person to ever get through in one lifetime. Bring in the friends. Rejoice in what they are contributing. Their ideas, creations and ways of handling sticky situations are there for you to experience. Listen to their stories. Laugh along with them as they relay a joke heard at work. Check out their vacation pictures. Get movie critiques. When you attend an event together, enhance your experience by hearing what they got out of it. Have a potluck, taste new-to-you recipes.

Good friends enhance an inspired life:

- Surround yourself with friends who are positive.
- The people we have around us should be guiding us away from the storm.

- Lament your predicaments with your buddy. But, only for a *short* time The longer you stay in quicksand, the harder it is to climb out.
- Trials, tribulations, and stumbles can be crushed quicker with friendly advice and comfort. A listener with a warm cup of tea and a hug. Words said at just the right time. Or silence, nods, understanding. A good friend knows what you need to get through a difficult time.

The best way to attract tip-top friends is to be one. Peace, pleasure, laughter and loyalty. Traits that you want to be around come from within you first. As Gandhi said, "Be the change you wish to see in the world." Switch up the words and become the friend you want to have.

Experience, solve, and lift one another up. It's what healthy friendship is based on.

Originator As Leader

Leaders have original ideas. This may sound like an obvious assumption, but when I heard it, it rocked my world. I'd always thought of leaders as charismatic, outgoing, loving the lime light; qualities that don't come naturally to everyone. But original ideas, we're all born with those.

Thoughts for our inner leader:

- Ideas don't have to be momentous, or life changing ideas. It could be as simple as a new way to prepare fruit, change a tire, tie a shoe lace, wear a scarf, stretch muscles.
- Leaders set the models, so make yours based on love and truth.
- Others may follow you. Without tripping, keep an eye on the trail you're leaving behind.
- There are a multitude of ideas already in the world. Use them (without plagiarizing, of course). Take those concepts and create from there. You didn't make the

personal computer, but you can use it to write a blog, contribute to social media, conduct research for an innovation.

- Watch out for past leaders. Whatever they were dealing with may be different from what is essential today.

- We all have filters on that guide our viewpoint. If you're following one leader, you are subject to only his slightly skewed vision. It's when you are learning from a multitude of people that you can form your concepts more accurately.

- "An expert in a field is someone who is ten miles away from his house," my college professor used to say. Leaders are given that role often because that's how they're perceived. It doesn't necessarily mean they know what they are talking about.

- Whatever you present to the world, there will probably be someone who will benefit.

You are a leader because you have original ideas. Your leadership is crucial to the creativity of the world.

Make Something Appealing

Creative projects are splendid when they're appealing to *someone*. Seeing another appreciate your gift to the world gives that notorious warm and fuzzy feeling. Remember:

- Projects don't have to draw in everyone. Getting a smile from one person, an appreciative snort from an animal, or just pleasing for the creator, can be enough.
- Appealing is subjective. 'One man's trash is another man's treasure'. So don't fret if few people dig your dirt.

- If it charms you, there will likely be someone in this world who will like it, too. Think of our huge world population.
- Giving and receiving starts with being a giver of something that someone else enjoys. Your art piece, music, popcorn seasoning recipe (I have a great one!), whatever you have to give, give it.
- Don't worry about it being too weird. Once a friend and I stumbled on a museum about serial killers. Okay, sounds creepy, but it was fascinating! Their upbringings were all horrific. Brought interesting discussions about why most people can survive horrible childhoods while others are affected so profoundly. Whomever thought up that museum brought out deep

subjects that gave us something to learn from.
- It's easy to share creativity on-line and connect with millions.

If someone feels more joy, laughter, entertainment, or fulfillment from your creation then they will have benefited, and so do you. Create, and pass it on.

Original Bliss

Creating can put you in touch with the bliss that is within, slipping away into a feeling of heaven. Time and space disappear. There exists, for you, only the creation and you as the creator. You are in the flow. Present to the moment.

Picture yourself playing an instrument:

- You don't have to be the originator. In a musical piece composed by someone else, there exists the possibility of making it your own.
- No one else can play it exactly like you are.

- Feel the notes floating through you.
- Disappear into the sound.
- Be that music.

Constructing, you are ripping apart the chains that so often confine us to negative, stressful vibrations of the outside world. Shedding skin like a snake to your inner core: beautiful, abundant, joyful, and at peace. The more often you can get into that feeling, the more it will seep into your daily life. Enjoy!

Experience Enhances

Every situation you've found yourself in is something to add to your art. Encounters, travel, overheard conversations, good and bad times. Like tools in a tool belt, your life is filled with experiences that enrich your life.

- The senses are heightened: sights seen, noises heard, scents smelled, fingers touched, taste buds evoked.

- Past challenges can make similar ones of today easier to overcome.
- Every one of your experiences is important: the good, the bad, and the ugly. They may all be used eventually.
- Adding to your toolbox is automatic, without thought.
- Whatever has elapsed need not be cornered off into some sealed compartment in your brain, it should be used like a favored spice.
- It is accessed without knowledge, flowing through like a melting river of snow down a mountainside. There is, actually, no way to hold your past out of what you create. Your views are filtered through your past experiences and will be transported unconsciously.

So, be thankful for all that you have experienced. It can be used to heighten the art that is your life.

You can also use your past purposefully. Think of a recent chance meeting. Is there something learned that can be added to your creation? A writer often jots down overheard conversations, phrases uttered by friends, sentences that are heard on the radio. Then she takes those words and forms them into a story, or character dialogue, or to describe a scene. Conjure up for yourself anything that could be useful from your own memory. It's called a memory bank for a reason. It's there for you to draw from.

You don't have to have been a pirate and traveled the seven seas to create. It is more about recognizing the richness of what you are in contact with daily. Look around the room you are in. What colors are present? How many shades of red, yellow and green? What shapes do you see? Can you stand in a different way and take them in at an altered angle? Close your eyes and engage the other senses. Make this a habit, to feel the lushness of your everyday life as an addition to your creativity chest.

Know who has the most experiences? Elders. Too often older people are overlooked in our society. Our culture tends to think of them as having less to contribute. But it's the opposite. The benefits of their lifetime of experiences can give wisdom that can make us better people. If we truly listened to them about the horrors of past wars it would make us less likely to do anything to bring about another. My grandmother, Frena, lived through the Oklahoma Dust Bowl. She has taught me the importance of never throwing out food but to always search for a way to use it. Listen to your elders. They have a lot to say.

Port Cities/Trade Routes

For centuries, cities with ports open for trade flourished in money, innovation, and variety. Townsfolk learned from the visitor's different ways to do things. Ideas were exchanged that could improve lives. Innovations spread like spilled syrup.

Markets became a place of seemingly endless spectacles: spices, silk, linens, cotton, food stuffs, teas, coffee, entertainment, animals, languages. Everywhere creativity was enhanced from the fresh perspectives of the visitors. Locals contributed their knowledge with newcomers.

Being alive today, with the world so open to trade, we have the benefits of gaining from so many different cultures. We are not limited to only the teachings of our own tribe. This learning from other parts of the world has been going on so long, it's not something we think much about now. But we were once stuck in the muck of the village viewpoint. The gaining we have from thousands of years of trading has made variety a way of life. The diversity of resources for us to draw from extends from one end of the earth to another. And it was all formed long before we were born.

What started as the great variety of land and sea trade routes has now extended into the internet. Social media, phone apps, video chats, blogs—communication is instant. Research, business, agriculture, fashion—anything you want to know about is fingertips away. It wasn't that long ago that I did college essay research at the library. I don't think my sons have ever opened an Encyclopedia.

Being a creator now, we are spoiled in multiplicity. Excellent time for us creators to be born!

Like compound interest, a rich life gives more original ideas.

Chapter Two
Don't Sweat--You Are Already Creative

Your life is a personal toolbox overflowing in creativity. It holds unique, custom-made items. Pick and choose which tools you want to use to bring the joy of inspiration into your life. You own a mighty big toolbox.

We Have Pushed Our Boundaries

Early humans migrated to discover new places. The reasons were many: overcrowding in tribes, natural resource depletion, villagers being outcast, or the desire to discover new terrain. Whatever the reason, traveling takes creativity. Land that is new to travelers will bring about new challenges. Could be different animals, food sources, weather, terrain. If humans were not creative, they would have died off, eaten by cunning predators or starved because they couldn't figure out new ways to procure a meal. There were no fast-food restaurants along the highway thousands of years ago.

They came up with a way to catch that bison, eat a turnip, crack a walnut, or went to bed without any supper.

But humans had a cunning tool— creativity. We could alter how nets were lined, change the shape of digging utensils, design better arrows. Adaptation goes with the human brain.

The need to migrate still exists but for different reasons. Harsh dictators, countries at war, governmental corruption, extreme poverty, and climate change. The people forced to leave their homes often face huge challenges in the places they end up. And, as their ancestors did, they eventually create ways to acclimate. Anything from learning how to cook new food items to opening a business in a new country, immigrants have learned to adapt.

If humans were not innately resourceful, we would have never been able to flourish throughout the world. Never doubt your ability to be creative—it's already a part of our species.

Abundant Abilities

You are a beholder of countless talents. You have the ability to create joyful activities, relationships, and a new flavor of ice cream. There are giant waves of potential waiting within you to sweep down and enrich your life.

Think of a composer of classical symphony music. His musical piece can use wind, string and percussion instruments. Within those categories are flutes, clarinets, horns, violins, cellos, harps, xylophones, and cymbals. From study, practice and talent, he can create a single piece of music that can leave people breathless in appreciation of its beauty.

You are a composer. The knowledge that you have accrued in your life has become your personal symphony piece. There is no bad, dull, gross individual song. If you decide you want your song to be different, change how you think about it. Think about what you do want. Then start making the changes to get there. Your expertise is wider than you may believe.

- If you are a parent, you have management skills
- A sibling, social skills
- A son or daughter, the ability to forgive your parent's shortcomings
- Friends, communication mastery

Think of your upbringing, schools, jobs, relationships, money situations, travels, home life. Everything around you brings something to learn from.

That knack for inventing is not only for the young in body. The ability to create starts as soon as we recognize it and plumps down on our couch to stay. It can be the elephant in the room that you ignore, or a welcome companion wedged into the folds of your brain. No one comes to us and robs away that ability. If you can

- Read this book, you can write your own
- Breathe, you can create new breathing techniques

- Clap your hands, you can drum a fresh beat

These are meant to be simple ideas that are a flake of an ice chip as to what you are capable of. Less than an ice chip, more like a lick. If you can swallow the idea that you are capable of creating at the most mundane, bottom of the bottomest pits, then your concoctions have nowhere else to go but up.

Future Faith

There will always be challenges in life that can be solved through creative ideas. If we didn't have faith in our abilities to solve problems through our own creativity, we would have quit this game of life thousands of years ago.

When cavemen got cold, they did not shiver to death in their homes. I imagine they noticed that the animals kept warm with fur or feathers. Since they could not grow their own, they hunted, skinned, and made themselves a warm covering.

Creativity got us through the days before clothing shops, indoor plumbing, and food delivered to your door. Our challenges both today and in the future may be different, but they'll still persist. Without even thinking about it, we know those new problems will be solved.

Right now, there are plenty of world problems: hunger, climate change, homelessness, war, corruption. My cat tells me that I forgot to feed her this morning—so not true. There are so many issues to deal with, it would be understandable to hide under your bed covers until they're all gone. But instead, we do the almost ludicrous thing possible, we get up and go on. We know that the problems will be solved and/or adapted. Changes will occur and we trust that we can figure it out.

If we stopped having a faith in survival, that would be a dull world. We also have faith that things will get better. Even when it's not obvious, there resides within us the understanding of an improving world. We may not be dwelling upon an improved life, but the background noise is always present, no matter how soft the sound may be. It is an undercurrent, like the tectonic plates pulling the continents along, or the oceans to not disappear overnight, or the black and orange caterpillars showing up every summer in our yard, we know that life is progressing.

Humanity has surpassed its history of the caveman era, no more grunting language for us.

Chapter Three
Meditate

Want to get something done? Ask a busy person to do it. People who are used to accomplishing many things are equipped to get it all done. Alternatively, lazy people find creative ways around work to get it done faster. A great way for both types of people to accomplish their goals is through meditation.

Meditation has a plethora of benefits:

- Allowing creativity to flow more often
- Getting us out of our roles
- Not being impassively shaped by our experiences
- Being open to new ideas
- Responding rather than reacting
- Opening doors to previously unthought of possibilities
- Teaching us to be present in the moment

Avoiding Negativity

Our naturally occurring, default state is love. When you meditate, you're activating those naturally positive, intrinsic pulses. It's like discovering your inner organs are really comprised of unicorns and rainbows—if those make you happy. Here are some thoughts on meditation:

Attachments: While reflecting on the beauty of the lotus flower, lower vibrations that have attached to you from outside influences are forced to drop off. They're no longer strong enough to hold on. Your inner love vibration trumps all others—it's the knock out winner!

Feeling low: When you have low energy, gaps or dips in it, it is more susceptible to picking up outside forces. Think of times you have been around people who are angry, fearful, annoyed. When you're in a great mood, it's easier to block their negativity. You may even bring them into your positive vibrations. But when you are also feeling low, you may begin to feel worse. Your physical and mental health can suffer. Allowing your mind to regroup and your body to relax is your built-in process to get back to your natural loving self.

Practice: If you are a habitual meditator, it's easier to reach that loving inner self. It's like taking daily, long distance runs before a marathon. When the big day comes, you're more ready than the person who has kept their exercise routine to strolls around the block.

Leeches: Have you ever been in a great mood, ready to cheer the world, and exuberating appreciation? And then, you run into someone and quickly feel depleted? You've been attacked by an Energy Leech. Their energy can suck out your healthy energy field. If this is a person that can be avoided in the future, do your best to stay away. Also, make it a habit to not hug or shake hands with people you've just met because that's a common way to get soaked up. If you do get swallowed, take a few mindful breaths. Recognize your eternal connection to the vast store of energy within. Bring it on and follow along with your day.

Mirrors: A tip to use when confronted with a negative person: imagine mirrors. Picture mirrors all around your body that look outward. When the person looks at you, they'll be 'seeing' their reflection. The negative energy that has been spewing out of them is now amplified by this reflection. They have their energy, plus the reflected energy. The most likely outcome is they'll want to get away from you—and fast. Use caution. If they're holding a gun or likely to get violent, don't play the mirror game. Their hostility could amplify.

Meditation is your shield against every day, contrary intrusions.

Inner And Outer Field

We each carry our own energy field, your unique vibration. It extends outside of your body from the crown of your head to your feet, then back up from within. Picture yourself as an apple, choose your favorite (mine is Red Delicious--mmm!). Your energy field flows upward through the core of the scrumptious apple, out through the stem, around the vibrant red or green peel, and then back up the core through the bottom of the apple. It is meant to be a non-stop process. When it's distorted, mind and body can be adversely affected by:

- Poor health
- Foggy attention
- Stress
- Anger
- Fear
- Negative thoughts

Meditation is an efficient way to bring back its natural, free flow. It is an un-blocker, a green traffic light, a highway that clears the lane for your car.

Your natural core energy is healthy, strong, love-based, and filled with abundance. It's made to deal with stress, illness, disease and negative influences. Wiped clean of the dust bunnies of piled-on, daily stressors, the inside of you is beauty, peace, contentment.

Three Beats Time Excuse

Having time to meditate can be a non-issue. You don't have to be a yogi master, sitting on a hillside, meditating life and chewing figs as you contemplate the meaning of life. Three mindful breaths can do it.

The catch in that sentence is the mindful. It means paying attention to the breath as it flows into, throughout, and exits your body. Just that little bit can pull you back into the present. Try it now:

Relax your shoulders and jaw.

Be aware of your natural breath entering your nostrils.

Notice that it passes down in to the lungs and belly.

It travels throughout your body without your having to guide it.

Your chest extends slightly.

Without pressure, it glides back out through nose or mouth.

Repeat two more times.

Do the mindful three-breath exercise each time you think of it. Do it in a stressful moment. Do it throughout the day. Pretty soon, you may decide to get wild and try out four breaths. Keep increasing those breaths. They are meant to be continued...

Do Your Thing

When my kids were little, there was little time for my own needs to be met. Their nurturing needs were a near constant. My breaktime? The bathroom. Shut the door, sit on the lip of the tub, breathe.

When my grandmother was raising her three kids, none yet in school, grandpa was away in the war. With no family members to help, no nanny, and neighbors just as busy, she was left on her own to cope. She found her break in the front yard. Leaving the kids in the house for a few minutes, she would escape by watering the lawn. In her words, "we had the greenest yard in the neighborhood."

A few minutes of daily meditative time may be where you are right now. If that is all that you can see your schedule dealing with, that is enough for change. It will improve your life.

Whether it be three breaths, bathroom escapes, or lawn watering, create a way to practiced mindfulness. It doesn't have to be a separate thing from your real life. Of course, if you can meditate for an hour or so a day, do it.

Fifteen Minutes A Day

Yes, I just gave examples of quick access meditations. As you discover the benefits, you'll likely want to do more. To fit it into my day, I set my alarm for half an hour before I need to get up. With the first alarm, I lie on my back, no pillow, and focus on each body part. Starting with the toes on the right foot, I travel up the leg. Next, the focus turns to the left leg. Then the fingers, arms, body from the bottom to the top of the crown. I focus on my breathing. I keep a mantra going through my brain. I slip into a meditative state.

This isn't for everyone. Many people have told me they've tried to meditate in bed and drift right into sleep. Maybe the lie down method could be a great way for relaxing into sleep at night. Let's discuss other options for you.

Sit in a way that is comfortable for you. This could be the traditional way of sitting cross-legged on the floor, or in a welcoming chair. Close your eyes (after you have read this, of course). Hands on your lap. Turn off cell phone ring. Make certain you'll be comfortable for a long stretch of sitting.

Here are three ways to use your fifteen minutes a day:

1. *Focus.*
   Concentrate on the stuff going on around you. Start with the most obvious, the things that are begging for attention. What noises do you hear? Hum of an air conditioner, neighbor mowing the lawn, washing machine? Listen for the quieter noises. Bring your focus closer to you. Take time with this. No hurry here. As you notice softer sounds, bring that focus closer to your body. Wind your way to you. Feel your lungs breathing in the air, chest

moving in rhythm. Ultimately, your destination is your heart. How is your body feeling? Tingling in your hands? If so, this is usually a sign that you are experiencing a meditative state. When you feel ready, let go of the focus on the stuff happening outside the body. When you feel like you're in the body, you're meditating.

2. *Mantra*.

A mantra is a phrase, poem, prayer that is repeated over and over again. It can be as simple as, 'God is...I am' to a Sanskrit verse. Christians use Hail Marys, The Lord's Prayer, or the Prayer of Saint Francis. Find a mantra that works for you. Keep it peaceful and memorize it. Get back into that meditation pose, silently say it to yourself. Over and over again. Focus on it, keep it, be with it. When you feel ready, it's okay to let it go.

3. *Breathe*

Follow your breath. Start with the usual flow of air. In through the nostrils, out through the mouth is a common way to start. Start to be aware of the breath as it travels through the body. Feel it glide through your lungs, belly, outer limbs, shoulders, neck and head. Now, forge your own pathway with the breath. Imagine it to be pulled from the earth through your feet. It runs along the front of the body, around the crown of the head, and back down. Let it absorb back into the earth and begin again. When are ready, try other pathways: from the right foot, up the right side of the body, top it out at the crown of the head and forge down the left side of the body. These pathways can go from arm to arm, leg to leg. Bring the flow focus down different body paths.

These are three techniques that take practice to achieve. Refrain from beating yourself up for not being a meditative master. Start with a goal of three minutes. As you master that, move on to five. Somedays will be harder than others. Be okay with that. Meditation is a time of self-acceptance.

As you are meditating, thoughts will come into your head. Don't judge yourself for thinking. Rather, be aware of them. Notice they are there. Be the 'outsider' watching these thoughts circulate around your brain. Watch as they leave. Go back to your mantra or breath focus. Even the masters get passing thoughts. It's when we focus on them, get annoyed with them, give them judgmental attention that they become more pervasive. Like a two-year-old in a temper tantrum, wait for it to be over. Resume meditation.

Projects as Meditation

Projects or hobbies that are quiet, peaceful and take little thought can put you in a meditative state. I've heard mixed reviews from support to opposition in this as a form of meditation. It may not be under the strict definition of meditation, but a hobby that absorbs you is just a shade away from traditional meditation. The benefits can still be felt.

Mine used to be cross-stitching. I had to stay focused on the stitch. Quit paying attention and it's easy to screw up. My mind was tied. Thoughts held to what I was doing.

Think of a project that you can do that will melt into your everyday life. Visit a craft or hobby store. Search the internet for ideas. Ask friends what they do. Could be weaving, gardening, painting, tai chi. Whatever you can do that is quiet, peaceful, absorbing, and gives you joy.

Ways to meditate can be creative. Don't think that the traditional ways to do it are the only ways. Adapt it to your life.

Intention Based

Before meditating, you can set an intention for something you want. You can ask questions, such as what are good ways to:

- Attract friends, finances, a lover
- Have a more fulfilling career or retirement

- Bring forth ideas for a business project
- Be a better parent
- Serve humanity
- Find purpose
- Be more healthy
- Enhance creativity

Give a *few* moments of thought to what is troubling you, no more. Ask for clear, easy to understand guidance to solving it. Then, let it go. Surrender your issue to the feet of Goddess, your angels, loved ones who have passed before you. They know a heck of a lot more solutions than you could ever fathom.

The answer may come during your meditation in the form of images, direct 'downloads' of what to do, or ideas you had not thought of. The solutions you hear could also be something you don't recognize as solutions. You could hear something like: forgive those who you believe have wronged you, love more, accept help. Chances are the answer to your issue will come in a way you don't expect.

Or, you could hear nothing at all. This doesn't mean that Plan C is not going to be given. Keep faith that if you have asked, you will receive. It just might not be answered in that moment.

Your answer may come in something seen on the internet, heard on the radio, or overheard in line at the grocery store. Recently I asked what I could do to increase sales while I was driving home. I happened to look over and saw a huge banner on the side of a building, "Build Your Reputation". There was my answer.

Goddess created a plethora of options. Choices are an everlasting buffet. Rely on this fact and work with her to create the plan that works best for you.

A side note: Setting an intention for another person to do something doesn't work. Just like you, they have free will. Keep your desire to what you want. Row your own boat.

Respond, Don't React

Meditation helps to lead us to the more efficient way of dealing with challenges by responding; reactions are reduced. This does not include needed physical reactions.

Reactions happen without thought. They're automatic. If a lioness crosses your path, a reaction may send you running. The hunt is on. Unless there's a jet pack attached to your back, you'll likely be her supper. Reactions are ideal for removing your finger from a hot stove, but fatal if you become easy prey.

Response comes from wisdom, it's creative and comes in the moment. It allows you to step back from a situation and assess what the best choice is; to come up with a creative, fresh solution. It's being utilized when thought has been allowed to wedge its way between a stimulant and an action. The lioness is the stimulant, your quickly thought-out, plan of action is your response.

Other examples:

- If someone cuts you off in line at the grocery store, a reaction pushes them to the floor and stomps on their egg carton. A response politely lets them know the line is behind you.

- If an acquaintance tells friends that you starve your children, a reaction is to shove her face in cake. Responding is to tell her to stop the rumor mongering.

- If someone at work is stealing your lunch, a reaction is to throw rotten tomatoes in his face. A response is to send out a memo that your lunch will periodically contain salmonella laden sandwiches.

Overindulging To Reactions

Lionesses don't normally cruise down the street, waiting to charge when you step out of your house. A more common stimulant is to feel like you've been insulted, injured, or harmed. Working through these challenges with a caring friend or therapist can help with the healing process. But when the problem becomes an obsession that is dwelled upon, stress and health problems can result. There are three common reactions:

1. *Heated confrontation.* One person going after another, justifying why you're right and they're wrong. While this may serve the ego, it does nothing to solve the situation.

2. *Holding onto anger.* Stuff it down like a hot chili into your heart. This is the one that is most likely to cause health problems. It also often bubbles up as passive-aggressive behavior, adversely affecting relationships.

3. *Self-Gossip.* Spending countless hours telling friends all about your horrid experience is its own addiction; one I've struggled with. This can be a splendid unifier for friendships but is not a healthy place for your spirit or body.

Staying away from those three common reactions takes time and practice. Better to focus on beneficial ways of response. When you're ready to respond to the party that you feel injury from, here are some steps to take:

- Do a love check-in with yourself
- Take three deep, mindful breaths
- Avoid being passive-aggressive or sarcastic
- Be sure that you are seeking a peaceful outcome
- Focus for a moment on your heart, allowing it to open
- Block negative reactions from the confronted person

With a prolonged habit of meditation under your belt, you are more likely to respond to situations rather than react. Meditation gets you in the practice of having a clear mind. You're less likely to be hindered by thoughtless reactions. Responses are given precedence.

Don't ask me for an appropriate response to a lioness attack, though. I have no idea how to handle her charge.

Chapter Four
Tell Your Tale

Your world is created by the stories you are telling yourself. They come from those around you, life circumstances, upbringing, interpretations, and experiences; a culmination of your life. Wrap yourself in appreciation of your life story—it's where your delicious creations get their ingredients from.

Reality Show

Every day you are in Season One, Episode One of your own reality show. All of them are original. What makes it unique is what you choose to see. No one else is perceiving it with your senses, understanding in exactly the same way.

I can look out a window and tell you about the lavender blossoms that were exploding last week in the yard but are now shriveling from an excessively hot summer. A roommate may look out the window and note the dog poop a thoughtless neighbor left in the yard. Someone else may be fascinated by a vintage car parked down the street. We all have a different way to share the same view. How we present the same window scene is creative because it's from us.

You have the choice to make your show whatever genre you wish: drama, comedy, romance, childish, action, adventure, horror, survival, spiritual growth, or fitness. It's not what's going on in your life, but how you're experiencing it. Your feelings about daily life come from within and you have control of that.

For tips on directing your feelings, refer back to the chapter on meditation. Also, I recommend reading *The Fifth Agreement* by Don Miguel Ruiz and Don Jose Ruiz.

Non-fiction Creativity
Truth in creativity keeps to what *needs* to be expressed to tell your personal story. This means telling what happened in a way that others can understand. No adding

embellishments that divert away from whatever relevant message is crying out to be understood. For example:

- Adding extra notes to a musical composition can make it a dud
- Not chipping enough of a sculpture is like tossing blankets over it
- A work memo with meandering gibberish causes workers to glaze over the message

One of my favorite sentences in a novel is in *Tender Is The Night* by F. Scott Fitzgerald, "The hotel and its bright tan prayer rug of a beach were one.".

Not one word in that sentence is not true. Fitzgerald says all that is needed to pull us into that beach. His beach to rug description used simple words that brought understanding. The fun part is the creativity of how he put the words together. He was telling his truth with precision.

Telling exactly what you see or experience makes your life easier by:

- Not needing to change a story later
- Not stressing over remembering exactly what lie was told
- Being someone people can trust
- Having an effective, efficient communication style
- Being able to accomplish projects more quickly because you are simply telling what you're seeing, feeling, experiencing

This isn't going against Expressionism, Abstract, Cubism, or Modern Art. Dali's melting clock painting needed every brushstroke to complete the feelings, emotions, and message that he was trying to convey. He was telling his truth with exactness.

Tell the story that needs to be told with clarity and get out of the way.

Other People's Stuff

When you ask questions and listen to what people have to say, you're going to hear some fascinating stuff. Their stories can expand your repertoire of subjects to know something about, correlating into more to add to your creative pursuits. And as Aunt Judy used to say, "I already know my story. What's happened to you?".

Everyone has a history, and most enjoy sharing it. Be the instigator of people's anecdotes. The topics are endless:

- Childhood
- Career
- Parenting
- Run-ins at the grocery store
- Traffic
- Family
- Cooking
- School

I remember years ago sitting down to lunch in the cafeteria with a new co-worker. She was quiet, I didn't know anything about her. She was sitting alone at a table. Politeness compelled me to sit with her but my brain was screaming that this would be a boring lunch. Thankfully, I was wrong. After a bit of coaxing, she told me of growing up on the family Christmas Tree farm. Her father in the off-season was a kind, gentle soft-spoken man. But come harvest time, it all changed. Every family member was put to work. Dad became a Jeckell and Hyde, yelling, scolding, punishing. The siblings worked hard at cutting and packaging the trees for shipping. They were in constant fear of punishment. But the day the last tree was sent out, Dad went back to his loving self.

Talk about a story! The harvesting of Christmas trees, a family farm, a contradictory father, living far from neighbors. Wow, quite an entertaining lunch.

Had she only mentioned that she had grown up on a farm, her life story wouldn't have kept my attention. She started the conversation only when I asked open-ended questions.

Open-ended Conversations

Questions that leave room to be answered beyond yes, no, maybe, whatever, or fine, are open-ended. When I asked my new co-worker where she was from and she answered up-state New York, that could've been the end of our conversation. We could have continued slurping soup and twirling pasta. But I kept at the questions. Did she always live there, what was her childhood like, what kind of farm did she work on? From this tactful, gentle prodding, the story came out.

Here are some suggestions:

- Keep your questions on the path that the talker has laid before you. If the conversation begins with what happened at work that day, don't skip to what movie they saw last weekend.

- Give time to hear an answer. Just as nature abhors a vacuum, conversations dislike long pauses. Ask a question, listen for a response. If the response is extremely brief, patiently wait a few more seconds. Often, the speaker will fill the gap with more talking. This is often where the stuff gets good.

- Don't ask a question and then wait for the pause just so you can blurt out what you have to say. This is their time, not yours.

- Listen. You know you're listening when you forget what your next question or comment was going to be. It's listening in the present moment, leaving out expectations, that stories come forth.

An added bonus to asking open-ended question is that people will be drawn to you. In our busy society, being heard is a big deal. We all want to connect. Be the one who starts the game of connection, and you will gather friends.

Three Conversation Cautions

1. If you practice open-ended questions, you need to have the time to listen. As in, 'how are you' as you rush past before an answer can be heard, there's no expectation of an actual answer.

In high school, our drama teacher gave us this exercise. When passing fellow students in the hall and a friend calls out, "how are you," answer that you have a week to live. I tried it numerous times with the same results: no one stopped to address my answer. Taught me that if I'm going to ask something as casual as how someone is doing, I will be asking because I have the time to listen. Otherwise, I keep my greeting to 'have a good day'.

2. Non-stop nothing talkers: the ones talking zilch out loud, they just want a person in front of them with the ability to hear. How do you know they're talking about nothing? When your attention keeps slipping like a

kid with too many birthday presents. Another tell-tale sign is that the dull speaker won't acknowledge your input. When this happens, here's what you do: tell them that you need to leave, move on, talk with someone else, or throw your face in the punch bowl.

I once had a friend who called to talk quite often. While I enjoyed hearing from her for about ten minutes, I grew tired of the chatter. But I did like her. So, I started every conversation with a time limit. "Great to hear from you. I have ten minutes to talk." At the end of the prescribed time, I was resolute and said goodbye.

3. Keep mindful that if the talk turns onto topics you find negative, repulsive, contradictory, or offensive, you don't have to put up with it. You can: try to lead the conversation to more neutral grounds, change

the subject, say you don't want to talk about that topic anymore. If the person persists in the offense talk, say goodbye and leave. Unless you're chained to a chair, don't burden your ears with ugliness.

If you try and convince an offensive person they're wrong, chances are it will lead to your ego chirping off to their ego. Confrontations like this generally don't turn out well. Accept that you feel differently, and move on.

Same City Adventurers

People who have lived and traveled in many places are often thought of as having a more compelling life. But equally fascinating can be people who have lived in the same area their whole lives.

I went to eight different elementary schools, two middle schools and six high schools. No, I wasn't a naughty kid repeatedly expelled; each new school went with a household move. I've lived in three different states and four countries. I didn't live in the same house for over two years until I was in my thirties. This leads to a curiosity of what it would be like to have lived in the same house for an entire childhood. Even more thrilling are people who never left their hometown when they became adults.

Getting to watch the people and places change over the years is a treasure chest of creative knowledge. Nothing stays the same. Comparisons can be made that have stature. Knowing the life stories of those around you gives a fullness to your story of them. Same goes with the place, home, and city. Same people have read the whole book of their region, not just the page of the day.

Those same-city folk born in similar time periods would have diverse stories about the same events. Mutual friends would be described contrastingly. And every one of their stories would be original because the storyteller would be reading from a different angle.

Rethink assumptions of those who stuck with the same place they were born.

Their wisdom is deep rooted. If you're one of them, examine your everyday life. This way of living has a relevance to it that is subtle, don't skip over the contributions that aren't as readily seen.

Experiences Shape

Creative thoughts are influenced by our past. It creates a filter over your everyday thinking that is almost impossible to avoid. Ideas, no matter how original, have been glazed over like a feather dipped in honey by what we have encountered. Viewed in a positive light, this can be a good thing.

Ask yourself some questions like what:

- Part of the world were you raised in?
- Are the family stories you hear at gatherings?
- Wild things have you done with friends?
- Obstacles and challenges have you encountered?

- Life changing events have you gone through?
- Ordinary, daily stuff have you met with?
- Experiences have shaped how you see the world?

No one else has the same answers to these questions, the same clay. You don't have to worry about coming up with a new way to shape a vase in a ceramics class, it will automatically be different through your hands.

Your past has an inherent beauty to it. Cherish what is yours and yours alone. You get this autobiography and no one else. It has probably been fraught with a combination of pain and suffering, joy and peace. But whatever it has held, it's yours. Use what you have encountered to construct what only you can.

Travel

How your viewpoint and creativity has been shaped by your life experiences isn't easy to see on your own. It's like asking a fish what it's like to live in water. But having more resources than a fish, you have more opportunities to figure yourself out.

Traveling is a great way to understand yourself, *if* you seek to learn from the different culture. I've witnessed U.S. citizens in other countries demanding, even shouting, that locals speak to them in English. Sounds crazy, but it's true.

When you travel:

- Be open

Accept that other cultures have ways of handling things differently than to what you're accustomed. Remember, you're there to learn, not to press your mode onto them. Grasp what others think, how they do things, how they interact. Other cultures can be fascinating when you are willing to be unbarred from your standards.

- Laugh

Jokes are funny when a norm is broken. So, when you don't share the same norms, the jokes can be nonsensical. It's okay to ask what is causing the laughter. What are you missing that would make the giggles work for you? Most people will enjoy getting you into the fun. Laughter is most often invigorated when more people are sharing it.

- Note the gap

Note the differences from your home base that can enlighten you to things you take for granted. An Irish visitor asked me how we have hot water first thing in the morning. I was dumbfounded with a question of something I had taken as a given in every home. Turns out in Ireland, the first person awake turns on the hot water heater. It's a way to save on electrical costs.

- Ask

If you know the language or have an interpreter, ask locals what they think of people from your country. If you're from the U.S., many people believe we're all living the rich life, straight out of a mansion, and that we hang-out with movie stars. Also, their views on our government can be highly enlightening.

- Don't judge

Every country has negative issues. As Jesus said, "let he who is without sin throw the first stone". Wherever you're from, nothing there is perfect.

There's something I would like to add about traveling. While I felt enriched from learning from other cultures, there were instances when I did not. Animal cruelty, racism, human oppression, violence is not justifiable because it's from a different culture. In traveling, I've heard that excuse. Slavery was once part of our culture, and that never made it acceptable.

Friends

A good friend 'gets' you. If you have someone who can give a realistic critique of you, ask them for it. When considering who to ask, think about this: If you wouldn't take advice from them, don't take criticism from them.

How we come across to others is invariably different than how we think we are. Ask your friend for the truth, but to be kind. Some structure for them to follow is this: Tell all the positives about you, and then what you could be doing better. End with suggestions for improving.

When you ask, be in a good place with yourself. Don't do it after getting home from a crappy work day and fierce traffic, or you may bite the head off your friend. Stay calm, relaxed and ready for self-awareness.

There will be things you disagree with. But often, those disagreeable things may have a grain of truth in them that you hadn't recognized. Sometimes it takes a while for you to accept that grain of truth. Progress doesn't happen overnight.

Just because these are things coming from a friend, doesn't mean they're completely true. What can be the case is that you weren't aware that some part of your behavior isn't coming out as intended. Knowing how others see you can be an opportunity to ensure that how you are expressing yourself and how others take it is closely aligned.

While you are hearing your friend out, you have one big job:

SHUT UP!

If you interrupt, you're probably going to try and defend yourself. That's your ego talking. You are welcome to disagree, but do so silently. Now is the time to listen. Because again, it's not always about how you are, but how your behavior is being perceived.

At the end, of the talk, you're free to ask questions. And again, be ready to learn from the answers.

Assumptions

Assumptions are based on guesses, judgements, filtered viewpoints, and past experiences. As such, they may or may not be true. The farther you get away from assumptions, the closer you get to reality.

We make so many assumptions every day, it can be like fleeing from an Olympic runner in trying to get away from them. We assume that babies are cute, there's a man's face on the moon' and eggs are for breakfast. However, not all babies are cute--my dad says I looked like Nixon. Many Native Americans see a rabbit on the moon. Eggs are in quiche, a night time meal.

When a sculptor transforms a block of marble in to a work of art, she's chiseling out what is hidden within it. It's revealed through her work. Same as you stripping away your assumptions. It's getting to this core, this hidden sculpture, that your creativity is lurking.

Become your greatest sculptor by:

- Detaching from your assumptions
- Seeing without judgement
- Looking on without emotion
- Studying a situation
- Zooming in and reporting on what you see with real life goggles attached

Assumptions hide reality. Creativity comes from within you, not your assumptions. Assumptions cloud our thinking, our viewpoints. Peeled off, truths are revealed. The core of truth is where true creativity lurks. If you are assuming something, you are not being open to what could be possible.

How Others Treat Us And How We Treat Ourselves

When you see yourself as not worthy, ugly, goofy, or a dud at parties, your behavior will reflect this. You'll act outwardly as you feel inwardly. If you think of yourself as shy, you may not ask for a piece of cake at a birthday party. Giving up birthday cake is serious; it could be the greatest cake ever baked and you'd be missing out.

Also, negative images projected on to ourselves don't stop at our borders; they spill over to the outside. People pick up on our negativity and mirror it back to us. They may act worse when you're being a downer. And, you'll attract people with a less savory outlook, energy, integrity, and way of being. Your negativity will fuel theirs, throw more fire on yours, until the thoughts swirling around you will be a wildfire too hot to control.

There are tricks we can use to claw out of a well of a negative self-image:

- Fake it 'til you make, as in, pretend you're in a good mood and you'll eventually end up there
- Wear more flattering clothing
- Take a one-day class
- Walk through a park
- Garden
- Listen to and watch birds
- Get a radically different hairstyle
- Pick up a new fitness routine
- Dive into your bucket list
- Practice good posture

Doing things that cause you to feel better escalates. A focus on health that produces a healthier body will improve your self-image. A better body may cause you to want to wear clothes that highlight your new shape. Looking in the mirror and not wanting to run away screaming can motivate you to meet more people. Fun times, friends and laughter will be sure to follow.

Self-image also makes a difference in how we treat ourselves:

- When you feel deserving of respect then you will treat yourself with respect.
- Trustworthy, trust your decisions
- Reliable, rely on yourself for support
- Healthy, make healthy choices
- Honest, accept what you have to say
- Belonging, ready to contribute to any situation
- Compassionate, be gentle in thoughts and actions

As you become more self-confident, you're more willing to share your ideas and creations. Your creative additions are what the world is waiting for. We benefit from what you have to share.

Sharing your creations takes courage. It's taking what you may care deeply about and being ready to hear people's reactions. You may feel vulnerable, exposed. Having an inner core of high self-confidence helps to accept criticisms with grace. To understand that not everyone will appreciate your creations.

Treat yourself as the awesome being that you are. Goddess created a wonder in you.

Be in charge of your story, not the other way around. Your creative expressions depend on you being in control. And, I thoroughly recommend keeping it a story that you are happy with. Why not? It is your story, after all.

Chapter Five
Imagination, Play, and Curiosity

Imagination, play, and curiosity go together like identical triplets; it takes a bit of scrutiny to see their differences. Imagination is play of the mind. Play is taking action to that imagination. Curiosity is a yearning of the mind to play, with a splash of imagination.

<u>Imagination</u>

Imagination must be fostered, exploited and practiced. It is a force-fed thought, gently guided like a herd of wild horses running through a wide canyon. Imagination is a step into a realm of the brain that is freed from the roles that absorb us. It allows us to relax, take a breather, step out of the worries of the world.

Image a tropical island paradise:

- Close your eyes
- Feel of the gentle breeze caressing your skin

- See the colors of the birds-of-paradise flowers
- Dip toes into the warm sand
- Sip the luscious pina colada from the hollow pineapple
- Hear wave rhythms along the shore

Could you be snorkeling, and come across a mermaid the size of your hand? What would she look like? Would she belong to an underwater city built of braided sea kelp and decorated with tiny shells? Any adorable mermen around?

This is not the same as when your brain repeats the same information to you, caught in a repeat cycle. When you want to flex your imagination muscle, and that repeat cycle catches you unawares, watch the thoughts flow through your mind. Without judgement, watch them drift off and get back to your imagining. This is what I mean by force-fed thought. You have to keep your attention on your imagination. If you don't, your thoughts are susceptible to falling back into a repeated story.

A minute or two is all it takes to rip your mind free of the auto play of something yucky you heard from a co-worker today. You have a quick and easy tool to take back your mind and return to the joy that is inherent within you. Use it.

One Enhances The Other

Imagination and creativity are best friends forever. Now that you have imagined a new, mythical, underwater world, you can use that imagining to create something. How about a wide glass bowl with blue glass pebbles on the bottom? Add some mermaids fashioned from tiny dolls. Decorate with sea shells. Have fun with this. You may have just invented a new hobby for yourself.

Your creation doesn't need to be imagination first. Perhaps you like mosaics and want to create something unique. Gather crazy things that you could put in one: chips of mirrors, old brooch, silver lighter case, skeleton key. Don't stop with what you know would work, or have seen before. Get ridiculous. A piece of zipper, glass vial and thermometer, buttons, cabinet knobs, light bulb, old earrings. Now you have the idea of what you want to create, with a pile of wild things to fill it with.

Do you think the creator of the peanut butter and jam sandwich thought of this masterpiece without first getting wild in thought on what would taste good with those mashed peanuts? Likely, their imagination got a little crazy and thought up all kinds of food partners. Who would have thought those two could create such a tasty staple lunch? Would not have been my first thought had I never heard of that combination. It took imagination and creativity to bring you the PBJ. Tasty partnership of imagination and creativity.

Use Wait Time
Imagination is like a muscle that grows weak from non-use. Be on the look-out for ways to use it. If your head is almost consistently focusing on the practical, the

imagination will dry-up like a neglected house plant. Keep that muscle strong—use it!

I wrote a story about a three-inch-high girl who lived in a pepper tree, *What Piper Peppertree Found.* The idea came to me at a fifteen-minute traffic light that I endured Monday through Friday. At the corner was a large pepper tree. What could be happening between the long hanging, leafy branches and the trunk? What could be living in there? Like the deepest depths of the ocean, the ideas as to what could be going on in there were unlimited. Like—a family of tiny people. Hence, the creation of *What Piper Peppertree Found.*

Use wait times to flex imagination muscle. Let the questions creep in. Transform your time from an annoyance to an opportunity. In line at a bureaucratic office with the service creeping along like a slug? Make-up stories about the people in line with you, the more fantastical the better. Stuck in traffic? Imagine what every carload of people are doing at home that night. Again, get crazy with your thoughts.

There are opportunities at every red stop light to bask in the frivolities of the imagination. Just, don't forget to move forward when the light turns green.

Healthy Play

Play is imagination in operation. It sparks up into acting out through games, free-for-all dancing, swinging in the park with your kids. What is your play? If the thought of doing it forges a smile, that's your jackpot.

According to helpguide.org, playing can:

- Lower stress
- Improve memory, think memory games
- Make you more productive
- Help develop and improve social skills
- Enhance your relationship: Couples who play together are more likely to stay together
- Keep you feeling young and energetic

- Heal emotional wounds
- Teach cooperation with others

All that, and it feels good.

Play In Childish Spirit

Visualize children playing. What are their emotions? Joy? Enthusiasm? Delight? Most likely there will be eruptions of laughter. These positive emotions release endorphins that relieve stress and anxiety.

Exactly what you need.

When my boys were young, we had a house rule that you were not allowed to walk around the house with a box on your head. As you can probably guess, it stemmed from them breaking things as they plunged around the room, not being able to see, arms thrust out in front of them, box knocking over whatever lay in their path. It still brings me laughter, the thought that this had to be an actual rule.

No need to partake in the same activities that kids do. Play can be a puzzle, card game with friends, paint and wine night, or a board game. Anything that you enjoy. It's not what you're doing that is of utmost importance, but that you're having a good time.

Don't think of play as a luxury for vacation time. Reverse that thinking in to part of your health regime—as important as exercise.

All Work

A friend who owned a busy coffee shop was asked when he was going to take some time off to make some money. Immersed in his business, he had bubbled himself into only seeing what was going on in the immediate environment. His mind was too occupied to allow for experimental ideas. Blocked by the sight of the tree, not stopping to see the forest.

How can you have those financial ideas that will rake in barrels of money if your head and body are focused on the daily grind? If there are no breaks from work time, there are no breaks for creative acceptance time.

Being bombarded by work is a trap, a fish bait, a focusing carrot.

Engaging in play away from work frees the mind. Step back, take a brain break. Clarity comes when we are refreshed.

When you're at work, remember to not get bogged down. Low-key merrymaking can add some pep to your step. You'll not be stuck in the muck of experiencing the daily routine as a bore. Bagging groceries can be like a puzzle, fitting in the food items into the bag like a big block puzzle. Writing office memos can become a game of balancing what needs to be included with how few words you can get away with constructing. Pretend you're an undercover journalist, acting like you 'work' there but are really about to break out a big story about the company you work for.

Shifting your thoughts from another humdrum day to one of play can amplify joy. When you are happier, fellow workers may treat you with more kindness. The day will go by faster. Your days can be more fun and interesting. Being playful doesn't mean nothing gets done, but it does bring more joy.

Housework is wide open to play. Wiping off counters could be you versus the death causing germ. Vacuuming in patterns can turn your vacuum into an artist tool. Cleaning out a closet could be a search for gnomes.

Play gives a space for those money-making ideas, and adds joy to the daily grind.

Playful Present

When you add play to your life, you are enlisted in the present. You have to be focused. If your mind is drifting off to some worry or concern, you'll lose the game. You must be present to win.

This is especially true when being creative in your play. Now, not only are you playing, you are adding original thought. Double whammie. You get to come up with new ways to frolic.

So just think about how wonderful it is that being playful takes us away from daily challenges. It's like a mini vacation, anytime you want. Hop out of the way of nagging guilt, frustrations, anxiety by being captured in fun. Sounds of laughter sound rather smart.

Friendly Play

Friends are not just in your life to bring chicken soup when you are ill, water your plants as you jet off to Hawaii, or hug in times of crises. They are there for laughter, fun, and play. It could be:

- A weekly card game
- A stitch and bitch event
- Daily walks that involve gossip and laughter
- A group meet of half an hour chanting
- Bolly dancing
- Easily made music with hand drums, shakers, or tambourines
- Lounging on the couch sipping tea or mojitos
- A light potluck
- Making vision boards
- Laughter yoga

- Tai chi

Friendships can keep us happier, lighten our load. When you go for a pedicure with a friend, it's the joking around that can make a routine toe trip more enjoyable. Add to that a favorite iced coffee and the remainder of the day will be heightened.

Friends were made for fun.

Friendly tip: When I put together a weekly meet-up at the beach for friends and our kids, consistency helped. We met at the same place and time every week. People knew we would be there. We had both a steady following, and some who occasionally came. Keep this in mind and see if you might want to become a playful host.

<u>Body Appreciation</u>

You have probably thought about how thankful you are for health. We're all at different lines on the ability to move, energy levels, strength, and flexibility. Wherever you are on the scale, be thankful for your body. It is a wonderous gift. But, just saying thanks is only part of the equation. It's using that body to whatever extent you can that shows it why you're thankful.

The body is not meant to be appreciated as a concept. It is the using of it that is the key to keeping it going. If you want it to know why you want it to be healthy, use it in a healthy way. Dance, walk, hike, play frisbee golf, or throw a ball with your kids. Show that body why you are thankful for it. Engage in healthy play. And if you include a friend in that dance, you are combining laughter, body appreciation and play into something even more grand.

Bliss of Curiosity

There's so much hype about working in your bliss, it can feel overwhelming. As in, 'What if I don't have anything that grips my attention so hard, I lose track of time? What if there are no 'in the zone' projects in my life?" The saying goes, 'Follow Your Bliss and The Money Will follow'. Talk about pressure. Does that mean I can never make money?

No, it doesn't.

Replace the word bliss with curiosity, and the weight is off.

Curiosity is easy, you don't have to follow an all-consuming life path to get it. There are no learning fees, apprenticeship applications, or major demands on your time. And, there's always something to inquire about:

- How does your phone work?
- What is that distinct, delicious herb in your sauce?
- How do turkey chicks know to follow their mother?
- What would it be like to be a billionaire?
- How would it feel to use a pottery wheel?
- What would make my picnic basket easier to carry?
- What would it be like to golf?

Think of things you've been interested in but have yet to try. Then, explore. Take a cooking class, play a round of golf, cruise the internet. Within your budget and ability, try out what you want to know more about. Keep it casual, fun, pressure free. Who knows, something might wiggle its way into becoming a personal bliss. But no worries if bliss eludes you. Curiosity is enough.

Impractical No More

There was once a young woman who was taught by her mother that to cook a turkey, the sides had to be cut off. The bird was carved into the shape of a square. The young woman questioned this. They decided to ask the grandmother. They called her and she said it was the way her mother had taught her. The three of them took a trip to the nursing home where the great-grandmother lived and asked her why the turkey was carved into the shape of a square. The old woman laughed and said that, being poor, she owned only one pan. It was in the shape of a square. So that was how she shaped her turkey.

So often, we keep doing what we've been doing even if it's impractical. Relying on what we've been doing, or what everyone else is doing, we don't look to thinking of new ways to try something. There are often more advantageous solutions. Keeping your mind at the ready like a mountain lion ready to pounce will surely produce some practical answers.

Some practical tips:

- Question what isn't working smoothly for you
- Ask if you have to put up with the annoyance
- Give yourself time to relax and think of new ideas
- Allow for silly or outlandish notions
- Write down your thoughts

Okay, now you've got your grievance and some solutions, even the outlandish ones. Is there something in your notes that could be used to fix the problem? A seed to work from? If so, use it; try it out. If not, be on the lookout for creative solutions to float your way. Answers have a way of wriggling into your attention and being heard. Just like my fat, black cat—when she wants fed, she doesn't stop crying until that food bowl is filled.

No matter how long something has been done a certain way, generations or centuries, doesn't mean that's the only way it can be done.

Knowing Nothing

When you start to learn a new subject, you may think you have an understanding of it. But the more you know about something new, the more you will probably realize that you don't know so much. Rather than shying away, use curiosity to propel you into learning more.

At the Naval technical school I attended, we learned about electricity. As with most people, my curiosity was flat when it came to electricity. I turned on a switch, light came into a room. What else did I need to know? But when I learned about alternating and direct currents, I wondered why the currents traveled in different ways. After some great discussions with teachers, the truth finally came out—nobody really knows why. Getting down to the nitty gritty of energy, vibrations, electrical flow, wires, wireless, there is a lack of a definitive explanation. Wow, not even the experts really know. Talk about a great subject to be forever curious about.

As you investigate your interests, be ready to be hit with the realization that you don't know much about common things. There's always more to know. This can mean that your chosen subject will forever provide you with a source to learn more from. There is no dead end to research. Fascination is always around, waiting to entertain you.

Many Subjects

Knowing more about many subjects gives more tools from which to create. The more you learn, the more things that can add to your inventions. Life is not about knowing only one subject, it's variety that gives the zest.

Be curious about your self-knowledge. Make a list of subjects that you know a bit about. Once you start it going, you'll be surprised at all the knowledge you've accumulated over the years. Everything on that list can be harnessed into whatever you want to give life to. You may already know:

- How to start a campfire
- Best route to avoid traffic
- How to get your partner to laugh
- Most pliant clay for bowl making
- About kites from the Middle East
- Where to buy mung beans for fresh spring rolls
- Type of sage used in smudging
- The difference between a spade and a shovel

Pat yourself on the back. You know so much more than you give yourself credit for. Every speck of wisdom you have stored away has the potential to add to a creative project.

Creative Crafty People

There are people all around you doing different activities. Take the time to ask them questions. Very few artists and craftsmen are against the idea of sharing what they know. Ask:

- A weaver how their loom works
- A printer about the history of P's and Q's
- A ceramics maker about kiln differences
- A glass blower how they got started

Don't stop with questions directed to what you're already interested in. Gaining knowledge about any subject can be more interesting than you might have thought. Who knows, it might even drive you to want to learn even more about the subject.

Imagination, play, and curiosity radiate all the more with creativity added. Keep your life joyous by plugging them in wherever you can. It's why we are here on earth.

Chapter Six

Self-Imposed Blocks

Unless enlightenment has been achieved, the blocks listed in this chapter are in all of us. Our goal is to seek out this inner gunk, face the blockage, let it go, and fill it in with creativity and love.

Accepting Your Truth

Figure out your inner gunk by getting to know yourself. What are your preferences, viewpoints, feelings, and emotions? Much of what we think we know about ourselves is tied like a leech to those close to us. They often tell us what we are like. Have you heard you are shy, aggressive, loud, cheerful, slightly stupid, clumsy, or hate eggplant? Once you have heard these traits many times, it's easy to attach them to yourself. This puts your personality into someone else's hands.

To get out of that strangling hold:

- Question your beliefs, making certain they are your own
- Meditate, asking to be aligned with only your energy
- Try new things, seeking to discover fresh interests

Be pragmatic about who you are right now. As you discover yourself, be willing to face some stuff that you may view as negative. Have you been harboring jealousy, anger, or racism? Engaged in gossiping, holding grudges, vanities, or showers of self-sympathy?

Letting go of your unwanted aspects involves non-judgement. When you can understand that those aspects are not tied to you like the lungs you need to breathe with, then you can understand that they can be let go of. It's when you give them your emotions, thoughts, or too much focus that they stick to you.

As you ascertain your unwanted aspects, chip them away. You are your own sculptor. No one else has the privilege of defining you. Picture yourself with sculptor tools, carving out the real you.

Be sure to cover those in tools in velvet. This is not a time to beat yourself over the head because you are not seemingly perfect. Rather, welcome who you are right now: imperfect in your eyes, perfect in god's view. Your true self is talented, chisel away toward authentic creativity.

As you walk your path, stay away from comparing yourself to others. No one is alike. We are all on our spiritual trail. Thinking you're superior to someone else dirties your ability to see that we're connected to one another. It also makes it okay for someone else to think they're superior to you. Leave everyone else alone. Tend to your own garden, that's more than enough to work on for many life times.

People have their own path, their own self-image that has nothing to do with you. In turn, your past choices are your own. We tend to overplay what others think of us. Others are more worried about themselves then what is going on with us. You're rowing your own boat.

Filling yourself with love is not the challenge that it may seem. The love is already present within you. What you are really doing is re-discovering it.

Your Self As An Obstacle Course

Do you question whether or not you are a creative thinker? Think that title only applies to the brilliant artists making millions from their artistic endeavors? Or anyone living in the edge of society creating as yet undiscovered works of art and spending every waking hour tied to their passion?

Dash that mode of thinking from your mind. We are all creators. Questioning your connection to the creative thinkers of the world is a false thought. It's your mind blocking you from the reality of the situation.

You've probably heard that you're your biggest obstacle to success. That it has much to do with self-confidence and a fear of the changes that success brings. Whatever the reason, taking a deep breath and tentatively stepping into uncomfortable situations can bring incredible rewards.

Once I met a friend at a coffee shop. She was finishing up a non-fiction book. When I asked her about the book, she told me that after our time together, she was going to a class to teach the book she was reading. No, she had not read it before. She had confidence in her ability to teach and comprehend that book right before the lecture. Having known her for many years, I knew that her students would learn an effective, thought-provoking subject from a great teacher.

Are you ready to jump into a classroom and teach a subject that you've just learned about? I know I'm not. The thought of doing so makes me want to run away as fast as a writer racing to a book sale.

But you are an expert at something. Can you:

- Look after a child?
- Type on a keyboard?
- Pack a bag of groceries?

Then you can rethink how each thing is done. Creativity is not just for artistic endeavors. If you can take even the most mundane of tasks and change it to suit you better, you are using original thought. Altering something as seemingly insignificant as your keyboard position so that it suits you better, you are being a creative thinker.

Okay, now you've jumped that crack in the sidewalk. You are now entitled to think of yourself as clever. Do a happy dance, roar your acceptance speech in your head, acknowledge that goddess did not stick you in a plastic bubble made specially for the non-clever nerds.

As a self-accepted creative thinker, what else can you create? My grandmother always made certain that our meals had different colors. No plates of cauliflower, mashed potatoes, and white fish. She would have switched that cauliflower to broccoli, adding a splash of green, with a lemon wedge on the side.

Picture ways that you have already done things in an innovative manner. Validify your past self as already being an original. It makes it much easier to expand your creativity when you know that you already are creative. Keep your mind open and keep at what you have been doing. Each time you try doing something in a way that is new to you, smile at yourself. Keep it up and keep going. Being creative is you, being you.

Guilt Tripping Trips You Up

Feeling shame or guilt for past behavior is a self-retribution. It allows us to feel that we have served a punishment for a crime, a penance. Guilt is like a mental whip that we use to inflict upon ourselves. Once we have guilt-whipped our back, we may feel like we paid the price. Okay, I felt bad about what I did. Now I'm free. But that allows us to offend again. We paid our fine by feeling bad.

I'm not suggesting that we never feel bad about our actions. But rather to let those bad feelings quickly transfer into natural, healthy consequences.

Guilt at its base is having committed an offense or crime. It is a simple recognition that something was done that shouldn't have been done. That's it, nothing more. The problem is that we tend to let the guilt pull us down. We feel bad for having committed a crime. It's adding the negative emotion to ourselves where the problems start.

Wallowing in shame can feel physically painful, induce stress, and hamper our health. It can be worsened when people around us encourage our guilt. When they say, "I can't believe you did this. How could you? After all I've done for you?" We've probably all heard that before. And, even said the same.

What to do if you feel you have done something wrong? First, own up to it. Next, take responsibility. Finally, rectify any damages done.

Own Up To Your Misdeed

When you discover that you have done something wrong, state how you could have done things differently. This will prepare you for what to do in the future, and allow you to let go of that nagging, nasty guilty feeling.

Whether we are talking to ourselves about a perceived crime, or telling someone else that you feel you have wronged them, say this, "I did/said something that I feel I could have handled better. Here's what I'll do next time it happens."

And next time it happens, deal with it how you said you would. This approach opens the way for you to handle that next time with creativity. Our next time will be met with a new way to handle an old problem. Focusing on guilt keeps our mind looping on what we think we did wrong. It does not allow for a creative solution.

Stress

While shame is a thought regime set in the past, stress is in the present. Every moment in life there is something that could be stressed about. If you don't believe me, watch the news. But I sincerely doubt there are many people reading this who can't think of something to stress about.

When we're stressing, we aren't open to inspirations within. Think of each stressor as an annoying fly that repeatedly wants to land on your face—bzzz bzzz bzzz. You're so immersed in batting it away that any other thoughts are ignored. The more flies in your face, the less you're able to deal with anything else. Whip out your fly swatter of inner peace and calm. Take some deep breaths. Recognize that stress isn't serving you, but that creativity can.

What is your stress? Pluck it out of your mind and examine it without judgement. How can you fix it? Is it something small like taking out the trash on a rainy night? Or big, like how do you get the rent paid this month? No matter how big or small, there are challenges in life. It's the attaching of negative emotions that exacerbates them. It's like this:

- Treat the issue for what it is— something to be solved.
- Do what you can to minimize or do away with it.
- Use experimental thinking, as in, what could you do differently?

- Be open to diverse options.
- Change your outer and inner dialogue. Rather than something being a challenge, call it an opportunity for change.
- Turn those uplifting thoughts into actions.

If the rent is looming large, could you: hold a yard sale, sale handmade gifts, tutor kids online? Perhaps you could be looking at the long-term and going back to school for a better career. There is always a way out. Our ideas are not stuck in a room with no doors or windows. Open your eyes and seek them out.

Stress is meant to be tamed. Use your gifts of analyzing, selective thinking, and being the creator of your life. You are your own situation solver.

Worry

We just covered the creative blocks of the past and present with guilt and stress. Now we move into the future with worry. Easy to slip into, and a slippery slope to escape. Worry wants us to dance with it, never let it go, feed our minds with all the horrid 'what ifs', lavish us with tasty, anxiety-ridden grapes. It can feel like being in the bottom of an empty well, sides oiled, no way to flee.

Except, there is a way to escape. All we have to do is feel around the well and discover the ladder beside us to climb out of the worry well. It is our creative hands that will find that ladder.

A possible way to get out of the well is to imagine the worst possible outcomes: When going on job interviews, I'd picture myself sitting down in front of the interviewer and hearing a chuckle. The interviewer would be reviewing my resume, pointing at it and laughing. Between belly laughs, they'd ask if I really thought I could work for them. That the thought of me even imagining such a thing was ludicrous.

After going through this scene in my mind, I would think to myself, 'well, I've been through worse things than that. I could handle that.' Then, I'd be ready for the interview.

This isn't a prescription for everyone. When I suggested it to a friend about to go on an interview, she gasped in horror. She told me that if she thought of something like that before the interview, she'd never show up.

Another idea is to detach yourself from the worry. Don't judge it. Watch it float through your mind like a dust mite and wait for it to leave. As soon as it does, replace it with an outcome you want to happen. Focus on that. Focusing on what you want puts you on the path to receiving that. Choose the positive foot path.

There are an infinite number of ways to use your creative mind. Take control of it at the first sign of worry. Harness it over to the side of positive, productive thoughts.

Stubbornness

Sticking to one point of view, one way of doing things, one solution, is like turning your body into a wall in an obstacle course.

As others put up ladders to climb over your wall, you remain stuck in your own way.

I once owned a children's clothing store, bringing me in touch with many pregnant mothers. The ones who were nervous about childbirth, caring for a baby, being a mother were generally the ones who did a good job. They were open to admitting that they were unsure of themselves. As a result, they consulted other mothers, read books, took classes—anything to feel more reassured. They collected a variety of creative techniques to handle a bawling baby.

It was the mothers who claimed to know exactly how to handle everything. The ones with all the answers. These were the ones I worried about. As one mother told me, "I cross-stitch, so I know about patience." Yes, I thought, you know about cross-stitching. But does your project scream at four in the morning to be worked on?

As expected, when I went to visit her a few weeks after the birth, her hair was asunder, house a mess, and bags under the eyes from lack of sleep. She had been stubborn in her belief that all would be easy and it wasn't. Had she been open to the idea that she might not know what to expect, she could have better prepared herself by learning more before the baby came.

What you are clinging to with stubbornness? What way of doing something is pulling you down like a refrigerator in quicksand? Is this serving your better good? What about the good of those around you? Are you happy with your mulish behavior? If you have an inkling of desire to let go, there are options.

First, figure out what you want. Get a firm concept on the desired outcome. To be happy, at peace, healthy? A better relationship, more money, to learn German in Vienna? (oops, that last one is on *my* bucket list, probably not yours).

Then, place that goal at the end of the proverbial tunnel. What are some ways get to it? Is there more than one way? Most likely, yes. Walking, biking, jet propulsion device strapped to your back.

Oh no! The way through the tunnel has just been blocked by a pile of old crates. Well, you could stand around and hope that you can get through before that goal dissipates. Or...you could find a way to climb, shimmy, and crawl your way to the other side.

The well-known 'secret' for the spiritually inclined is that you are not alone in ways to reach your goals. God, angels, ancestors who've passed on, are milling around waiting to help you. Ask, and you will receive.

Inflexibility can block novel ways to move forward. Don't be set on how to do something. There are other options, be open to them.

Messenger alert: the means does not always justify the end. Just because you want fish for dinner doesn't make it okay to throw dynamite into a lake.

Clinging To The Old
Are you a clinger? Do you start too many sentences with, "back in the day?"

Have you said that when you were that age, kids never behaved that way?

This clinging to the old doesn't start and stop with older people. People of all ages can be stuck in the belief that their generation is better: more depth in conversation, appreciation of art and culture, variety in music, or integrity in the workplace. Pretty much everything was better, back then.

Change is a constant. Nothing stays the same. Once upon a time, books largely replaced story tellers, cars took away horse related jobs, the cotton gin released many people from the toils of separating cotton from its seed.

And guess what? There's good and bad in every generation, every change.

New technology, ideas, and solutions to challenges both small and big are being created all the time. If you're only seeing the greatness of the past, you're missing out on the wonders of today.

I can complain about the overuse of smart phones, how much better it is to visit people face to face, and that computers are making us less creative. Or, I can relish the video chat with my son stationed in Puerto Rico, keep up a group chat with my family on my smart phone, and use this computer to write, advertise, and create great book covers. Cheering feels superior to complaining.

What ways have today's innovations improved your life? What do you have to be thankful for from life's remodels? Look around you and voice your thankfulness. Start with the electricity that gives you light to see these readings. Move on to the washing machine that keeps your clothes clean, the music that is available at the touch of a finger.

Are your concerns about how people conduct themselves nowadays? Albeit, there have been changes with the attention so many give to computer screens. But families still gather for dinner, two-year-olds still have tantrums, and teenagers still know more than their parents.

There are impressive things about the past that can be incorporated into today's lifestyle. But don't become mired in the illusion that the past was all great and the present kind of sucks. Pluck out the favored chocolates in the box of today's creative inventions. Blend them in with choice older candy recipes. Stick with the game of today, it's got some marvels to appreciate.

Self-Rejecting Dialogue

Putting yourself down can be subtle, especially with your words. Words are powerful. Saying things like:

- I keep screwing up relationships
- I'm just clumsy
- I'm always saying the wrong thing
- I need to lose weight to get a date
- I'm terrible at math

Each of these leads a negative self-image. If you call yourself clumsy, you will remain clumsy. If you say you are terrible at math, you won't get past the constant need of a calculator. Just as in the previous section on stress, you may need to change your inner and outer dialogue. Use words to describe yourself in positive terms.

Start listening to yourself. Anytime you hear that voice of yours dip into the pool of negative self-thinking, don't judge it. Giving emotion to it keeps it glued to you. Rather, see it as a balloon, drifting through your mind. Allow it to drift out of you and then replace it with something you like about yourself. The more often you do this, the easier it becomes. The more positive balloons you have, the less room there is for negative ones.

Anything that you've done that you dislike was done in the past. Creativity exists in the present. Loving yourself makes you more receptive to your creative ideas that contribute to the betterment of yourself, your community, and the world.

Chapter Seven
Societal Stagnation

There are stagnations to creativity infesting our society. Most everyone is held back in some way from full expression. Creative, positive expressions benefit everyone, beyond the creator. Communities are more enchanting when variety is prevalent. Limiting the creativity of a group of people harms us all.

Poverty Hurts All Of Us

Creating a joyous life is difficult if someone is lacking basic survival needs. How do you get a decent job when you live in a tent and don't have appropriate clothing for interviews, easy access to a shower, or a computer for a resume? It is far easier to introduce people to the wonders of creativity when fundamental needs have been met.

The world benefits from the contributions of all of us. So, here's where you come in. If you have the means to reach across the economic divide and help, I urge you to do so. Being of service to others can bring you an intense appreciation of all that you have. The joy of giving is real, not just a cute cliché.

- Poverty needs to be met with non-judgement. Blame helps no one.
- Encourage people to see themselves as part of their own recovery, a co-creator on the way up.
- With gentleness and being mindful of a needy person's predicament, it's possible to introduce the idea of creativity.
- Whatever the way out of poverty is, visionary thinking is a must. A struggling parent could form a band of other parents to create a cooperative of childcare, or exchange food items to balance out nutrition needs.

As innovative solutions present themselves, positive outcomes to what were once supposedly insurmountable walls can crumble. Be a part of the process.

Roles

When I was a beginning massage therapist, I came across a shocking discovery. Massage usually begins face down on the massage table. I couldn't see their face until about half-way through when the client turned over. Now here comes the almost creepy discovery... I often wouldn't recognize the person after they flipped. I wondered at my lack of short-term memory. Was I so spacy that I forgot a face after half an hour?

No, the answer lay in the deeply relaxed client; they had dropped their roles in life. They were no longer attached to the facial expression of a parent, laborer, baker, candlestick maker. Yes, role playing goes beyond how we act. It slithers over to how we hold our face muscles, it's that pervasive. Once these people were completely relaxed, their true expression came forth. They were free to be themselves.

Role-playing can hold us down. When we limit our minds to what is expected from ourselves and others, we impede the creative process. If you view yourself as your role, then you will primarily be open to ideas that someone from your role would think of. You will be operating in a self-imposed tunnel vision.

"Middle-aged moms don't create fashion jewelry for the Goth crowd." "Real men do not match their tie color to their socks." Yet, maybe you were into Goth in high school and would enjoy making jewelry like what you wore years ago. Maybe you want to liven up your clothing expressions with wild socks.

What roles do you play in life? List them. Pick up each role in your mind and try it on like an outfit. Each role has its own one. When you're wearing the outfit of one of your roles, is your individuality suppressed? If you're feeling held down, what can you do to strip off that uniform?

Here are some suggestions:

- Begin anew. Don't cling to how you've done things in the past.
- Stop and reflect how you might accomplish a task if you came at it from a different viewpoint. If you're a teacher, how would your student approach a new subject? As a worker, how about your boss? As a gardener, what attracts butterflies?
- Think of some things that you want to do but don't because you aren't supposed to. Challenge that stagnant, old way with a readiness to try something new. But, please, keep it legal. Don't get arrested in wanting to be creative.
- Make small changes. The next time you go clothes shopping, look twice at that shirt that may slightly fall out of bounds to what you are accustomed. Buy

it. Is there an ethnic food you've wanted to try but thought it would be too bizarre for your family? Take yourself out to lunch and taste the differences.

- Get out of your role expectations. Experience more of what life has to offer. There is a world of ingenuity that you can be a part of.

Incorporating role-dropping can be shifted into thinking about those around you. Do you have a house cleaner that you only think of as a cleaner? They have ways of doing things that you could learn from. The grocery cashier, your parents, police officers, teenagers, and baristas. Stop seeing only the role people play in your life. Recognize that that is only a part of who they are. They are filled with various thoughts, just as you are.

You're a far better worker, politician, caregiver, senior citizen when you're being your true self. Stripped clean of role limitations, the inner self is inherently original, loving and compassionate.

Disclaimer insert: I am not suggesting that serving in a role is automatically oppressive. Rather, it is important to be authentic in your behavior. Don't let expectations from yourself or others dictate how you should be.

Racism

Classifying a race of people as a certain way, subtracts from originality. Humanity gains from the conceptions of all colors. If someone has a better way of doing something, it should be the idea that gets the focus. If it's disregarded because of their race, the world is choked.

Visionary ideas don't flow to a select number of groups. It's a built-in party gift for all who attend a life on earth. Everybody needs to share their gift to get the maximum richness.

Think of the human creations that have brought the variety we have today. It is the interweaving of all races that has given us this diversification. It follows that the more mixture there is, the more colors can emerge.

Immigrants

Think how dull restaurants would be if we only ate food of our ethnicity. I, for one, cannot imagine a world without Pad Thai. Too sickening to dwell on.

Food is the tip of the ice berg. The variety that is brought to nations from the influences of incoming cultures extends into child-raising practices, medicine and healing, art, music, technology, fashion, spices, how to use a potato, and ways to approach God.

If you see something from a different culture that you disagree with, it can cause you to be thankful for your accepted way of doing it. Or, you can glean from it by taking those aspects that you like. You can mix and match, adding to your buffet.

Before shirking from migrants, look for the good they can bring. There is a park near a past work place that I walked through on my lunch break. Every weekend, Mexican American families gathered there: soccer games abounded, potlucks were laden on the tables, children swam in the bay. I remembered thinking how much we had to learn from these tight-knit families. They had traditions, family support, and a weekly stress reliever of food, games and laughter. Their closeness is something many families could learn from.

Albeit, there are also challenges to bringing in different cultures. Issues of providing healthcare, housing, and food can be costly. Language barriers can cause misunderstandings that may lead to violence. Locals may feel neglected if resources are being utilized to help immigrants that they think should go to them. These bumps in the road shouldn't be ignored. In order to keep a happy society, bumps need to be addressed.

Overcoming difficulties takes creative thought. We need to ask:

- What strategies and programs are available right now?
- What have other societies done in similar situations?
- What resources do the migrants already have, such as job skills or education?

Integrating new cultures forces us to design new ways of doing things. It is in pushing ourselves to doing so that we grow. Sticking to only our culture is a breeding ground for stagnancy. Societies have the opportunity to thrive when we seek to integrate new behaviors.

Stereotypes

This slides right in with racism and roles in its limiting attributes. Stereotypes include but are not limited to:

- Gender
- Age
- Education
- Sexual preference
- Political affiliation
- Ethnicity

Typecasting comes from beliefs held in homes, communities, friendships, social media, and news programs. They're passed down through generations. People who hold influence over us can leave us more prone to accept their stereotyping, such as doctors, teachers, and political leaders. It's difficult to block the bombardment of limiting viewpoints that saturate our lives.

There are societies that believe: a strong husband must beat his wife, elders are weak in the brain, women are frail, if you don't have a degree, you must be rather stupid. Republicans eat kittens and Democrats are out to stop you from eating hamburgers. Goddess likes my religion but is ready to send you to hell.

I heard a researcher say there are only two ideas common in all cultures: incest between close family is wrong, and murder without cause is also wrong. This means that all of the supposed 'truths' of each society is only true within that community. Do a bit of traveling and you will find this valid. When I lived in Japan, I saw the women doing much of the construction labor. In the U.S., it's the other way around. In Costa Rica, five-year-olds climb up palm trees and chop down coconuts with their machete. Here, Child Protective Services would be called for putting the kid in danger.

It can be argued that research backs up your prejudices. Like that there is more crime in poor areas and this must mean that the impoverished are more likely to be criminals. But peel back that criminal label. What societal factors are pushing people into crime? Systemic racism? Lack of decent paying jobs in the area? Higher stress levels that lead to people lashing out in violence and/or taking drugs to self-medicate? It also needs to be acknowledged that white collar crime is easier to hide. Stereotypes are often easy to refute with a bit of background checking.

As with your ideas of race, now is the time to notice the stereotypes. They creep out in the phrases we hear and speak. Stereotyping clichés are everywhere. Boys will be boys. Teenagers know nothing of the real world. Blondes have more fun (we don't—I am one).

It's like wearing a pair of glasses that filter in judgements before the brain even picks up on what's happening. Rip off the stereotyping glasses and see people for who they really are. Throw them on the ground and stomp on them with big, bad boots. See yourself and all humans for who they are. Life will prove to be much more interesting.

Sitting It Out

When we hear or view racial attacks or stereotyping comments and do nothing about it, we're still doing something. We're accepting the behavior.

It's like a relay race with racism or stereotyping shoved inside the stick that is passed from runner to runner. You can run the track with the stick, take the stick and simply hand it to the next person, or stop the run and show the runners what they've been holding.

Showing the stick of racism doesn't have to be loud and confrontational. If it's coming from a place of love within you, the runners may not feel forced to defend themselves. Non-violent actions are powerful. If you're lucky, they may listen to your words. Or, at least one of the runners will recognize the truth in your words.

Many runners will probably feel threatened. Egos are difficult to throw out. It takes bravery to call out what others are passing along. Being brave means feeling fear but doing it anyway.

Watch yourself if you call out something you perceive as wrong. Self-righteousness is another form of ego. Look inside and question yourself before speaking out. Are you questioning behavior so you look like the good guy? Are you judging another person based on your own viewpoints? If you feel love is present in your take of a situation, picture the other person as someone who may simply need a gentle reminder that we are all creatures of God.

When I was stationed in Japan, my running partner was a black woman. Once at the end of a mini-triathlon, I said something about the difference in Japanese athletes and white, U.S. athletes. Quietly, she reminded me that black people are U.S. citizens also. It was a gentle shake-up for me. Her easy, light correction was powerful. Got me much better than had she yelled at me and called me a racist.

Whenever you do something that speaks the truth, you are sowing a seed. People's beliefs are usually learned over a lifetime. Remain in the awareness that gentle confrontations are fruitful. You just might not see the apple tree that you have planted produce fruit for a long time. But with water, sun, and proper care, apples will come.

Love always prevails, it just might take a while.

Where Is Goddess?

Why all the blocks? If Goddess wants diversity, why not knock out these obstacles? Goddess can do anything, why doesn't she blow away our limiting views?

Because we were given free will.

With free will comes the ability to handle our own predicaments. When you make a choice and don't like the results, you have the free will to make better choices. We can choose but need to keep mindful of what happens as a result. There are consequences to our choices.

Holding yourself responsible for the outcome of your choices can be seen as a blessing or a curse. It's easier to blame God for the good and the bad. You can't be held responsible for a bad judgement call if God is calling the shots. Accepting responsibility for your life, or at least your view of it, is a huge jump into maturation.

Free will gives us unlimited opportunities to be a better person. That feels better than simply wiping your hands clean of a sticky situation and asking why Goddess didn't fix this.

There are other benefits to free will. You get to feel that inner glow of self-recognition when you like the result of a choice you made. There are many things to be thankful for that you have caused. My ex-husband and I chose to have children. Rather than staying focused on the injustices I felt during our marriage, I strive to find the good that came out of it—two wonderful sons. Not a day goes by that we don't feel thankful for that choice. What choices have you made that you are thankful for?

Self-love runs rampant when you tame the societal obstacles that can affect us all. And getting over these views takes deliberate choices. There is the choice to search out within yourself your limiting beliefs. Then, to drop them. Finally, to replace them by being unlatched to an open-minded way of seeing people for who they are. Each one of these steps are choices.

Chapter Eight
Now, Let's Create Something

"The journey of a thousand miles begins with a single step."

Before You Start

Before starting a project, ask yourself: what do you want to create? No matter the project, there needs to be a general sense of your end goal. Even abstract art needs some questions answered. Ask yourself:

- Is there a feeling you want to evoke?
- Something you want to teach?
- Is this a piece for your eyes alone?
- If you want others to see it, how will you go about presenting it?
- Who will be your audience?
- Is this a project for the joy of simply creating?
- Will it be used, such as a bookshelf for your office?

- Is your aim to let the project reveal itself?
- Will you use an outline?

I recommend having an image of what you want to create. Then, be open to whatever happens along the way. Often if you have no image, it can be overwhelming to stare at a lump of clay and not know what to do with it. But, if you can tell yourself that you're setting out to form a bowl, it's okay to plunge your hands in and start forming that bowl. If your bowl starts to resemble a wide vase, that's okay! You'll have created something and not have been so overwhelmed that you couldn't even touch that clay.

Having an awareness of what you want to achieve ushers in peace. Your attention can focus on creating, not the fear of a blank slate of nothingness. Now you're ready to go!

Truth Telling

I once took a class on how to write picture books. The instructor had us take our picture book story, cross out all adjectives and adverbs, and see what was left. "That's your story," she told us.

Creations are best when the truth of them is revealed. The fullness of a project is seen when everything that's not the sculpture has been chipped away. Ask yourself:

- Is this my ego talking, or my authentic self?
- Am I embellishing with excess gunk to hide a dull creation?
- Am I playing to an audience, over presenting my best work?
- Are you impressed with your work? Chances are that someone else will be, too (Likewise, if you're bored with it, others will yawn over it, as well).
- Have you gained something from the end result, such as insight, a lesson, or a heightened experience?

Don't worry about a lack of personal recognition. The art piece will give hints who the artist was. Even with the same ingredients, same recipe, same kitchen utensils, the end product will somehow differ from the other cooks.

We want to discover the creation, not be clouded by the creator.

Kill 'Little Darlings'

Being a creative person involves trying out new things. In so doing, you'll come up with stuff you fall head-over-hills in love with. But if you become attached to it like a child to a favorite blanket, this may become your 'Little Darling'.

In writing, a darling may be a phrase, metaphor, or simile that is believed to become the new catch phrase for the world; posted on memes for generations to come.

Except...

- That phrase may not fit with the article.
- It might be amazing in another story but distracting from the flow of this story.

- It doesn't make sense with what's been written.
- It's out of line in what I've been trying to capture.

This extends beyond writing. Any project is susceptible to a Little Darling. Say you're decorating a bird house. You have an image of painting on a cluster of grapes. You've seen the image in your mind, a cluster of fat grapes, purple, ripe, looking so luscious you can taste them. Trouble is, you're painting the bird house with a sea life motif and grapes would pucker under the sea. They just don't fit.

So, take a deep breath, hug that darling, and kill it.

Or, draw that grape motif into a notebook and use it to paint your kitchen cupboards with fruit along the sides.

Part of dashing a darling is the faith that creativity is unlimited. Your ideas, imagination and ability to create something new is not in the finite. The next great thing you bring about may be perfect for what you're doing now. It's the end project that's important, not the individual pieces that interrupt your work.

Don't Judge

1. Don't judge while working on your first attempt of a project.
2. Don't pre-judge the design of another person.

A saying attributed to Ernest Hemingway is 'Write drunk; edit sober'. When under the spell of creating, pausing to judge what you're doing can block fresh ideas from flowing in. Learn to accept that all ideas don't have to be set down perfectly the first time. Mistakes can lead to something that could end up working for you. If we stop to criticize what we're doing, those twists and turns on the path to an original creation will be cut off.

Also, be cautious about judging the creation of others. Just because a creation isn't what you're into, doesn't mean that you can't take away some aspect of it that you appreciate.

As with many people, I hadn't considered myself a fan of modern art. "I just don't understand it," I argued. Then I took a college class in Modern Art, and we were sent to view the outdoor artwork on the college campus. One of the art pieces was a ten-foot-high, blue chain link fence surrounded by trees. Sitting on the hill nearby with a good view of the fence, I challenged myself not to judge the piece. Just accept it. Try to see what the artist was trying to capture. After sitting for a while, a soft breeze tossed about the tree leaves. Looking through the blue pattern of the fence at the moving trees, I felt at peace. There was the predictable, familiar pattern of the chain-link and the blue covering on the metal. The green movement of the trees became enhanced by the stationary blue.

How did the artist know this was going to give such a gentle yet bold piece? It was something so simple that it was crazy to think that it would have the ability to bring immense feelings of tranquility. Had they stopped to reason away their idea, the thought would probably be that that was a silly place to put a blue fence. And had I pre-judged it, I wouldn't have had the experience of peace that still affects me.

Avoid judging your creation when it's a work in progress. There will be time for editing, revising and polishing later.

And with that, be careful about judging the work of others. You may be robbing yourself of the opportunity to experience the unexpected.

Revising, Editing, Polishing

Even with a strictly adhered to outline of what you want to create, the rough draft is often done with some degree of abandon. Unless you're James Joyce or Mozart, masterpieces are seldom completed in the first go-around. Delete buttons, erasers and more seasonings are often vital in the process.

When your initial try at a project is complete, walk away. Put it on a back burner until you forget its exact contents. Unless, of course, it's a timely piece that needs to be completed right away. If you have the time, leave it for a while. But do come back. There's a danger here of getting caught up in life and abandoning your creation.

When you return to your diamond-in-the-making:

- Look at it from the eyes of an outsider.
- Stand back, gaze, walk around it.
- What's your creation turning out to be?
- What needs to be moved around, thrown out, re-done?

It's at this stage you may discover that your project has turned out to be something different than predicted. What may have started out to be a vase, turns out it would work better as a pen holder.

Now it's up to you to decide if you want to completely revise it into something different, or keep the fundamentals intact. The amount of time spent on revising is in your hands. Go with what you instinctively feel works the best.

After revisions are done, time to move on to editing. Normally, editing refers to written material. Here, I am using it to mean anything that needs to be done to make it right for you. It's straightening out a line of yarn in a weaving, adding more orange to the poppies in a painting, changing the knobs on a cabinet. When you've done all the editing you feel necessary, stand back and look at it once more. Are you done?

Well, guess what: to the artist, a creation is never done. How do you know when to stop messing with it? When you're so sick and tired of working with it that you can hardly be in the room with it, it's finished for you. There is never a true end to any creation, be okay with this.

Finally, polish. Wipe the dust, tighten the screws, hang up that picture, eat your perfect cake.

Practice
Louis Armstrong didn't wait until performance nights to pick up his trumpet or sing, 'It's A Wonderful World'. He practiced, I

imagine, hours every day. Now, I'm not suggesting that you quit your job and spend the day working on your art pieces—unless that's your job. But at least brush into your projects several times a week, or as your schedule permits. As my creative writing instructor said, "A line a day".

- Find creative ways to squeeze out times to generate.
- Keep your artistic side easy to access.
- Think of it as a part of who you are.
- Be habitual.

The time you spend practicing can be minimal. Fit it to what works for you. It's more important that you are checking in on your art than that you devote your life to it. It's important to keep that scent of art alive. Visit it often, even if it's just for a moment.

Be Open To Learning

Yes, you are a natural born creator. But, that doesn't mean your stuff can never get better. If you fall into the trap of believing there's nothing more to learn then you're barreling toward stagnation and boredom.

If you're getting tired of what you're doing, learning something new keeps it fresh. Ideas to spark the knowledge bug:

- Take a class, in person or online.
- Get a learning app.
- Read a book or ebook that teaches you something new.
- Listen to a blog or audio.
- Seek out others with your interests to learn from.
- Visit a small business that specializes in your genre.
- Find an internet chat room with like-minded individuals.

Teaching what you know is another great way to gain more from a subject. In order to instruct, you can plunge deeper into research to be ready for students. This may reveal new innovations of which you weren't aware. Plus, working with beginners and watching them enjoy the experience can re-engage your appreciation of creating.

Use that creative spirit to find easy ways to insert learning: audio lessons in your car or at the gym, a reading device in your purse or briefcase, or take along a friend to a class—clears up your social calendar while you learn. Have kids? My son and I took beginning Karate together. I got fit and had something to write about for my blog. Whatever way you want to try out, keep it simple, easily accessible, and enjoyable. If you don't, it's easier to phase out of the new habit.

There's always a new facet to be learned in your artistic genre. How many different types of painting techniques are there? Wood working? Sculpturing? All you have to do is tap into the information that's begging for your attention. Get the zest back into your creative life, learn something new.

Showing Up Is An Action

Stories abound of people being at the right place at the right time. I read once about a man who was traveling in a storm and was in the need of a bathroom. Nothing was open save for a funeral parlor. When he went inside to ask for use of the facilities, the receptionist insisted he first sign the Guest List for a funeral. As he wrote down his name and contact information, he noticed there were no guests on the list. Later in the week, he was called by the funeral parlor. Turns out the deceased hadn't been a popular person, no one else signed the guest book. In his Will, it was stipulated that all of his money would be given to those who had signed the book. It was a lot of money. The bathroom man became rich from just showing up.

Be Thankful

When I was at an extremely low place in my life, I clawed my way out by choosing to be thankful. We were living in Central America, no governmental safety net, far from home, the hospital was hours away, and I had no idea of what was to come. I became so ill I had to crawl to the toilet to vomit. Awful time. I decided that I wanted to feel better, not just physically but mentally and spiritually, as well. From somewhere within, I was guided to be thankful. Crazy me, I listened to that inner voice. Looking around the room, I gave thanks for the food in the cupboards, a place to live, healthy children, a toilet to vomit into. There was a wild owl we watched outside every night, a gorgeous river we swam in, and howler monkeys to entertain us. Soon, my mood lifted and the world became more joyful.

Transfer this spirit of gratitude to your ability to create. What other species on this planet has our aptitude, and opposable thumbs to forge out ideas into manifestations? We can use our imaginations to solve to many challenges, hurdle obstacles, and be of service to others. We humans have an enviable gift.

Here are some ideas:

- Start before getting out of bed, putting the day in a positive light.

- End the day in thanks, ridding your body of built-up crud, and promoting better sleep.
- In a stressful moment, close your eyes and picture something you appreciate--zaps the strength out of stress.
- You can always be thankful for something—right down to your breath; the supply is unlimited.
- Keep a special place to focus on thankfulness.
- Thankful thoughts can be creative, get wild with them.

Just thinking of all that there is to be thankful for brings a joyful swelling to the heart. It is a reminder that no matter the ills surrounding us, better things are forever present.

Now that you have told the truth, thrown out your Little Darlings, let go of judgement, revised until you vomit, what you have left is authentically yours. No one in the world could ever have come up with what you made. No one.

Go forth and create.

www.ingramcontent.com/pod-product-compliance
Lightning Source LLC
Chambersburg PA
CBHW071857020426
42331CB00010B/2548